OUR NEW ZEALAND

Conrad Sims has been involved in photography for 26 years. As well as New Zealand, he has travelled and photographed in the United States, Europe, Mexico and Australia. His photographs have been featured in many earlier books, including *New Zealand Houses Today* (1988), *People, Places and Paddocks* (1987), *New Zealand: A Special Place* (1986) and *Buildings of New Zealanders* (1984). He lives in Auckland with his wife and two sons.

OUR NEW ZEALAND

Photography by Conrad Sims

David Bateman

FRONTISPIECE: The changeable weather brought about by the prevailing westerly winds reaching Auckland's west coast, provides many interesting spectacles like this rainbow.
PREVIOUS PAGES: Matauri Bay, north of Whangarei, with the Cavalli Islands behind.
BELOW: New Zealanders take great pride in being "do-it-yourselfers"; housepainting near Waihi, Bay of Plenty.

Author's Preface

When asked to write a few words about how I photographed New Zealand for this book, I felt that was almost as big a challenge as all those months I'd spent on the road. I'm a visual person rather than a wordsmith.

In accepting the challenge to do this book, I knew the only way I could successfully meet it would be by becoming part of the country. So I converted my van into a mobile home to live in and out of for about six months. My idea was to photograph the country from the heart of the people rather than from the perspective of a tourist passing through.

New Zealand is like a condensed version of all the rest of the world, always with something new to photograph just around the next corner. Waking up in the morning alongside a stream, listening to the birds and sheep, creates a strong earthy impression and one which is very distinctly New Zealand. The sounds and smells of towns and the country all make their own statement, and to capture the feelings they invoke was my challenge as a photographer.

Conrad Sims
Auckland, 1989

Photographs © Conrad Sims 1989
First published in 1989 by David Bateman Ltd,
'Golden Heights', 32–34 View Road, Glenfield,
Auckland 10, New Zealand

ISBN 1 86953 009 8

Typeset by Typocrafters, Auckland
Printed in Hong Kong by Everbest Printing Co. Ltd
Design by Neysa Moss
Cover design by Errol McLeary

North Cape

Doubtless Bay
Ninety Mile Beach   *Matauri Bay*
Kaitaia   *Bay of Islands*
          • Horeke

                    • Whangarei
                    Waipu Cove   Gt Barrier I

Kaipara Harbour   *Hauraki*
                      Gulf   • Whangapoua
Muriwai •   • Auckland   Coromandel Peninsula
Karekare •   East Cape
                              • Thames
          Ngaruawahia   • Waihi
          Raglan •   • Matamata
               Hamilton •   • Tauranga   • Mt Hikurangi
     Te Awamutu •   Whakatane •   Opotiki
                              • Rotorua
                    • Tokoroa   Gisborne
          Te Kuiti •
                                   • Taupo   • Wairoa
     Taumarunui •   *Lake Taupo*
                    Mt Tongariro •   • Turangi   Mahia Peninsula
                    Mt Ruapehu •   • Mt Ngauruhoe
New Plymouth •   *Hawke Bay*
Mt Taranaki •   Inglewood •   • Waiouru   • Napier
               • Stratford   • Taihape   Hastings •
     Hawera •
          • Wanganui   • Waipukurau
                    • Feilding
                    Foxton •   • Palmerston North
                    Levin •
Cape Farewell   • Masterton
          Golden Bay   Kapiti I
               Marlborough
          Tasman   *Sounds*
          • Motueka   *Bay*
          • Nelson   • Picton   • Wellington
          Blenheim •   Cape Palliser
                              Cape   *Cook Strait*
                              Campbell
Westport •   • Murchison
Cape Foulwind •   • Mt Travers
                                   • Kaikoura
Greymouth •   Lewis Pass
Hokitika •
               Arthur's Pass
                              • Christchurch
Mt Cook •
               • Ashburton
Lake Tekapo
Lake Pukaki   • Geraldine
Franz Josef Glacier   Twizel   • Timaru
Mt Aspiring •   Mackenzie Country
Lake Wanaka   *Lake Hawea*   • Waimate
Milford Sound
Homer Tunnel •   • Oamaru
Lake Wakatipu   Arrowtown •   • Moeraki
Fiordland   Queenstown •
               • Alexandra
          Lake Te Anau
                              • Dunedin
          Lake Manapouri
               • Gore
Puysegur Point   Riverton •   • Invercargill
Foveaux Str   • Bluff

               Stewart I

Southwest Cape

ABOVE: Boating, in craft of whatever size, is almost
universally popular in New Zealand. Dinghies on the
foreshore at Russell, New Zealand's first capital but now a
quiet town and a popular Bay of Islands tourist venue.
OPPOSITE: Yachts at Opua. The sheltered waters of the Bay
of Islands are suited to all types of craft.

Christ Church, at Russell, is New Zealand's oldest church,
built in 1842 when whalers and missionaries populated
the embryonic settlement of Kororareka.

LEFT: Yachts at Kerikeri, Bay of Islands.
RIGHT: Giant kauri trees are a unique attraction of the
north. They grow to 50 metres high and more than 2000
years of age.
FOLLOWING PAGES: Sunrise at Waipu Cove Reserve, south of
Whangarei.

At Waitangi, Bay of Islands, sailing catamarans and pedal
boats are available for hire.

ABOVE: The beaches are the prime destination for the many New Zealanders who take an extended Christmas–New Year holiday. Langs Beach, south of Whangarei.
RIGHT: Boating at Wenderholm, north of Auckland.

ABOVE: A view of the Bay of Islands and adjacent coastline from the north. The Bay of Islands includes eight large and many smaller islands.

OPPOSITE TOP: Formerly the home of James Busby, the first British Resident, this early colonial cottage in the Bay of Islands was the scene of the signing of the Treaty of Waitangi in 1840 and since then has been known as the Treaty House.

OPPOSITE LEFT: A typical lowland sheep farm at Horeke, Northland.

OPPOSITE RIGHT: Grapes are grown mostly for winemaking, an industry that has experienced much growth during the past ten years.

ABOVE: Keelers heeling to a fresh northerly breeze provide a
tranquil contrast to Auckland's commercial centre.
Aucklanders proudly refer to their home as the City
of Sails.
OPPOSITE: Whatever the weather, windsurfers are active on
Auckland Harbour — the windier it is, the more they seem
to enjoy it!

The annual Auckland Round the Bays Fun Run, held in March, attracts up to 80,000 entrants who run the 10.5 kilometre course from Victoria Park to St Heliers Bay. FOLLOWING PAGES: The waterfront and commercial centre of Auckland.

ABOVE: Clowns and balloons add colour to the annual Farmers Santa Parade in Queen Street, Auckland.
LEFT: The ocean liner Queen Elizabeth II is a regular visitor to Auckland.

ABOVE: Clowns taking part in a waterfront carnival to celebrate the launching of a new racing yacht.
RIGHT: An open-air picture gallery in downtown Auckland.

A Pacific Island family in their Sunday best. Auckland is
strongly multicultural, with Polynesian immigrants from
Samoa, the Cook Islands, Tonga, Niue and the Tokelau
Islands. Together with their New Zealand-born
descendants, they make up about one-tenth of the city's
population.

ABOVE: Windsurfers, Mission Bay,
Auckland.
RIGHT: Fishing from the foreshore in the
quiet suburb of Devonport, Auckland.

ABOVE: Sunset over Auckland Harbour.
OPPOSITE: Yachts can be seen racing on Auckland Harbour
every weekend, and often on weekdays too.

LEFT: Auckland's many public reserves include the farm
park of Motutapu Island, with idyllic beaches easily
reached on foot after a launch ride from downtown
Auckland.
RIGHT: A stream mouth at Karekare, west of Auckland, with
the surf club nestled against a rocky headland.

ABOVE: Fishing at Muriwai on Auckland's west coast, where rocky shore platforms provide excellent fishing for keen anglers.
RIGHT: Horse riding, Muriwai Beach. In total contrast to the east coast beaches, those to the west have black sand and a wild, bleak landscape which gives them a charm all of their own.

Motocross sport at the Howick racetrack, east of
Auckland. Many forms of motor sport are popular among
competitors and spectators alike.

Early morning rural scene, east Auckland.

ABOVE: Potato pickers, Pukekohe, south Auckland. The area's rich volcanic loam, mild climate and good rainfall, enable heavy crops to be grown for Auckland's produce markets.
OPPOSITE: A lettuce crop ready for harvest on the rolling south Auckland hills.

Rural scenes in the Waikato.
ABOVE: Poplar trees at Raglan, near
Hamilton.
LEFT: Ponies, Matamata.
OPPOSITE ABOVE: Three shepherds near
Raglan.
OPPOSITE BELOW: Drying out at Raglan motor
camp.

ABOVE: Schoolchildren waiting to give a traditional Maori welcome during a royal visit to Ngaruawahia.
LEFT: An ornate Maori house at Whakamaru Village, near Rotorua.
OPPOSITE: A cataract leading to the Huka Falls, a short distance down the Waikato River from Lake Taupo.

The central North Island offers a wide
range of scenic attractions and sporting
activities in close proximity.
ABOVE: Mount Ruapehu, seen here from the
fertile downs to the south, is an active
volcano and the core of New Zealand's
first national park.
TOP: Skiing on Mount Ruapehu (2797
metres).
RIGHT: Sailing on Lake Taupo, the largest
lake in the North Island, with the central
North Island volcanoes behind.

ABOVE: Alongside State Highway 1, south of Turangi, with Mount Ruapehu in the background.
RIGHT: Mahuia Rapids in the Tongariro National Park. The Park includes three major active volcanoes, Tongariro, Ngauruhoe and Ruapehu, in its 80,000 hectares of wilderness.

Pohutukawa trees
provide a vivid
splash of summer
colour on the
northern beaches.
Whangapoua,
Coromandel
Peninsula.

ABOVE: Pines planted during the 1960s in the Whangapoua State Forest help ensure the continuation of the country's flourishing timber industry. Whangapoua Harbour lies behind.
LEFT: Old railway carriages at Waikawau, Coromandel Peninsula, converted into holiday homes or 'baches' as they are known in the north.
OPPOSITE: Windsurfers at Pauanui Beach, on the east coast of the Coromandel Peninsula.

ABOVE: The Karangahake Gorge, near Waihi, was the scene
of goldmining in the 1870s and 80s.
OPPOSITE ABOVE: The fountain on the Tauranga foreshore.
OPPOSITE: Waterfront scene, Tauranga. The city of Tauranga
and port of Mount Maunganui are the commercial centre
of the Bay of Plenty.

ABOVE: Farmyard and barn, southern Hawke's Bay.
RIGHT: A colourful use for an old delivery van.
OPPOSITE: Hawke's Bay is noted for the quality of its wines, produced from grapes grown in the mild, almost Mediterranean climate.

A Te Aute College rugby team at afternoon practice.
Established in 1854, the school, in Hawke's Bay, is
one of the nation's oldest.

ABOVE: Visits to Maori *marae* are becoming increasingly popular with tourists and locals alike; nowhere else is modern Maori culture more evident. Whakamakaratanga marae, near Hastings.

RIGHT: A house in the Napier suburb of Moerewa, representing an architectural style popular immediately after World War II. Napier is known worldwide for its *art deco* and related styles.

ABOVE: Lowland sheep country near Stratford, south Taranaki.
RIGHT: Playing golf at Inglewood, near New Plymouth, with Mount Taranaki in the background.
OPPOSITE ABOVE: Exotic trees near Taihape.
OPPOSITE BELOW: The Wanganui, 290 kilometres in length, is New Zealand's longest river after the Waikato. It flows from bush-clad King Country hills, through the Whanganui National Park, to the west coast.

ABOVE: Rolling hill country near Feilding.
OPPOSITE TOP: Drafting sheep in a stockyard near Taihape. The central North Island is a major sheepfarming area, with some large sheep stations established since the last century and others mainly by returned servicemen from both World Wars.
OPPOSITE LEFT: Sheep being auctioned in the Dannevirke saleyards.
OPPOSITE RIGHT: Penned sheep await the auctioneer.
FOLLOWING PAGES: Poplars have been planted on this central North Island farm to consolidate a closely grazed hillside and reduce erosion.

A barn and wheatfield on the fertile alluvial plains near
Feilding are evocative of the American prairies.

ABOVE: The open plains near Palmerston North are dotted with shelter belts and farm buildings which provide contrast to the subtle yellows of autumn.
RIGHT: Schoolchildren at play, Levin.

ABOVE: Government House, Wellington, set in the city's luxuriant Green Belt, is the home of the Governor-General.
RIGHT: Wellington's Botanical Gardens are famed for the superb tulips on display every spring.
OPPOSITE: Summer flowers provide a vivid splash of colour among trees and phoenix palms in a Palmerston North park.

ABOVE: Outside the "Beehive", seat of the nation's Parliament, the statue of Richard John Seddon surveys the scene. Seddon held office from 1893 to 1906, making him the nation's longest-serving Prime Minister.

LEFT: Yachts of the Royal Port Nicholson Yacht Club at their moorings by the foot of Mount Victoria, Wellington.

Scenes around Wellington.
ABOVE: The narrows of Wellington Harbour are not
always so calm; the often stormy approaches to Cook
Strait have claimed more than 50 ships since the
1840s.
OPPOSITE TOP: Wellington's central skyline, dominated
by the Bank of New Zealand building.
OPPOSITE LEFT: Pipers practice for a parade in
downtown Wellington. The "Beehive" and Treasury
buildings are in the background.
OPPOSITE RIGHT: Old St Paul's in Thorndon,
Wellington, is the smallest wooden Gothic-style
cathedral in the world.

ABOVE: Yachts on Picton Harbour, in the
Marlborough Sounds.
LEFT: Canoeing on the Motueka River,
Nelson province.

ABOVE: A forage crop near Murchison, southwest of Nelson, is much appreciated by these recently-shorn sheep.
RIGHT: Large vineyards near Blenheim form the basis of a thriving wine industry.

Nelson is noted for its long sunshine hours, which contribute much to the region's productivity.
ABOVE: Harvesting tobacco near Motueka.
RIGHT: Aerial topdressing with superphosphate is essential to pastoral hill country.
FOLLOWING PAGES: The remarkable Punakaiki Rocks, near Greymouth, were formed from layers of limestone and mud deposited between 37 and 24 million years ago.

ABOVE: Fishing boats at Westport during
the summer albacore tuna season.
LEFT: Rain forest, South Westland.
OPPOSITE: Lake Ianthe, Westland.

ABOVE: The Poerua River, south of Hokitika, is one of innumerable scenic rivers flowing from the Southern Alps to the Tasman Sea.

ABOVE AND RIGHT: The Franz Josef Glacier in south Westland, first observed by Abel Tasman in 1642 and then by James Cook in 1770, has shrunk in size during recent years but remains a very popular tourist attraction.
FOLLOWING PAGES: Partly shrouded in cloud, Mount Cook is New Zealand's highest mountain, at 3674 metres.

LEFT: Mount Cook on a fine day, viewed from the famous
Hermitage Hotel grounds.
RIGHT: Tramping in Mount Cook National Park, which was
established in 1953 and covers 69,958 hectares.

Roadside scene, Fiordland.

ABOVE: The road to Milford Sound passes through the wide expanse of the Eglinton Valley.
LEFT: Mount Talbot (2117 metres) and the upper Hollyford Valley, near the Homer Tunnel on the road to Milford Sound.

Sunrise over Lake Te Anau, Fiordland, the largest lake in
the South Island.

TOP: Near Queenstown, the famous passenger ship *Earnslaw* steams on Lake Wakatipu, with the Remarkables in the background.
ABOVE AND LEFT: Arrowtown, a legacy of the goldrush days.

Mitre Peak, soaring out of Milford Sound to 1695 metres,
was formed by mighty glaciers which once covered the
land.

High country of the South Island.
ABOVE: An open tussock basin near Lake
Tekapo.
RIGHT: A shepherd on horseback near
Twizel.
OPPOSITE: Countryside around Queenstown.
FOLLOWING PAGES: Hay bales by the shore of
Lake Hawea.

ABOVE: Pukaki Canal, part of a large South
Island hydro scheme.
RIGHT: Willows and reeds surround the
shores of Lake Tekapo.

TOP LEFT: Holiday cottages, known in the south as 'cribs', on the bleak foreshore near Invercargill in Southland. The setting is reminiscent of Scotland, from where many of the original settlers came.

ABOVE LEFT: Loading a sheep truck, near Riverton. Sheepfarming is the mainstay of the region's pastoral industry.

ABOVE RIGHT: Grain silos and wheat under cultivation near Gore.

ABOVE: Container terminal at Port
Chalmers, Dunedin.
RIGHT: Suburban houses in Dunedin.

ABOVE: Otago University grounds, Dunedin. This university is the oldest in New Zealand, founded in 1869. The city of Dunedin is often referred to as the Edinburgh of the south as it is predominantly Scottish in origin.
LEFT: Mural, Dunedin.

Christchurch has a distinctively English
atmosphere and traditions.
ABOVE: Christ's College was founded in
1850 to provide a traditional English-style
public school education for the sons of
colonial farmers in the province of
Canterbury.
RIGHT: Children playing in the Botanical
Gardens, with the old Canterbury
University College, established in 1873, in
the background.

Christchurch is aptly known as the Garden City.
LEFT: Fountain by the Town Hall, near the centre of
the city.
RIGHT: Christchurch Cathedral dominates Cathedral
Square. Designed by British architect Sir Gilbert Scott,
it took 41 years to complete, finishing in 1904.